Disintegrate/Dissociate

POEMS

Arielle Twist

ARSENAL PULP PRESS
VANCOUVER

DISINTEGRATE/DISSOCIATE
Copyright © 2019 by Arielle Twist

FOURTH PRINTING: 2023

ARSENAL PULP PRESS
Suite 202 – 211 East Georgia St.
Vancouver, BC V6A 1Z6
Canada
arsenalpulp.com

The publisher gratefully acknowledges the support of the Canada Council for the Arts and the British Columbia Arts Council for its publishing program, and the Government of Canada, and the Government of British Columbia (through the Book Publishing Tax Credit Program), for its publishing activities.

Arsenal Pulp Press acknowledges the xʷməθkʷəy̓əm (Musqueam), Sḵwx̱wú7mesh (Squamish), and səl̓ilwətaɬ (Tsleil-Waututh) Nations, custodians of the traditional, ancestral, and unceded territories where our office is located. We pay respect to their histories, traditions, and continuous living cultures and commit to accountability, respectful relations, and friendship.

Cover art by Saige Mukash, a.k.a. Nalakwsis
Text design by Oliver McPartlin
Edited by Billy-Ray Belcourt
Copy edited by Shirarose Wilensky
Proofread by Alison Strobel

Printed and bound in Canada

Library and Archives Canada Cataloguing in Publication:
Twist, Arielle, 1994–, author
        Disintegrate/dissociate : poems / Arielle Twist.
Issued in print and electronic formats.
ISBN 978-1-55152-759-8 (softcover).—ISBN 978-1-55152-760-4 (HTML)
        I. Title.
PS8639.W57D57 2019   C811'.6   C2018-906214-2
                                            C2018-906215-0

For my brilliant siblings: Kelsey & Calen.
Remember, we are salvaged from fury and fire.

In dearest memory of Elanor Christina Florence Anderson Twist Law Kokum, you gifted me my words.

"*I am trying to figure out how to be in this world without wanting it.*"
—*Billy-Ray Belcourt*

Contents

Prelude

The night our kokum died,
my mother cried out in
another language.
I hear her break,
the cracking of burning wood,
like it was my own bones
between walls of mud and dust,
the structure, on fire.

I begin to become undone by the sound.
A rupture, wailing and tears
landing on purple tiles.
My ears know everything
in this house.
I beg my eyes to stop
making an ocean—
water and salt
fill the crater next to me,
as if this bed knows nothing but loss.
I weep into a space left unbodied—
I think I'll leave mine too.

Disintegrate or dissociate.
I will deconstruct myself,
and rebuild in her vision.

Dear White, Cis Men

Dear white, cis men,

objects of affection,
lust in a spiral of
confusion and self-doubt
about my own desirability.
Your attention, I crave.
Your validation, I need.

Because you are
the ones to decide
if I am fuckable
if I am smart
if I am worth love.

So that,
when you stop and
tell me to smile
tell me that I am beautiful
that I should beam for you
that I should thank you
graciously, and say:

Wow, you showed me the time of day,

I will.
Because I still don't know what you could do
if I don't.

Dear white, cis men,

with voices that boom
power and authority

demanding the respect
you would not give me

no matter how powerful
my voice booms

back.

With blue eyes
that see me as a novelty,

a fuck.

This exotic girl,
brown skin with
tits and a dick,
you think you can buy.
Black hair

that you will grab fistsful of.
When I say no.
Your lips telling me I want

IT,

as you scratch my thighs
with a salt-and-pepper beard,
your rough tongue that
tastes a body

I told you
not to.

Dear white, cis men,

who make me question:
Is being trans worth being killed?

when I could have died
from my own smooth brown hands
never worrying about
slaughter by white hands,
calloused.

Force-feeding me thoughts,
where I wish I had a body
you could rape

a body that won't
fill you with rage after you cum

a neck you choose
to stop choking.

Dear white, cis men,

I am the thing that you love to hate,
and you are the thing I fear the most.

D/REAM ME

I lost it.

Sixteen silken with
  durex play
        luscious flavoured
  lubricant.
Passion cherry,
       popping cherry.

PDR didn't prepare me,
          fail me harder,
Daddy.
      D/ream me harder,
             Daddy.
  My asshole wasn't ready,
      Daddy.
How does a fag get fucked
      without a fissure,
a cut?
      Without
         bleeding out?
'Cause what they don't teach,
     we learn in hospital beds
     on the bathroom floor
of every mall
       and every bloody toilet.

Arsonist

I was always content
with the scent of
freshly burned bridges
the way they crumbled
ash flaking
dissolving into air
as my mind sang
melodies of destruction
my throat well versed.

I build to bridge
gaps—void to void
structured
with flammable words
I will consume them
fill my lungs with tar

burning by my own flames.

Prairie Beneficiary

My   trust fund
was   a   legacy
of   violence
against   bodies like
                    mine.
My skin leaves me destitute
this blood, aching and hungry.

Not That Girl

Rupture   my
vocal   cords
for   I will ask
who   will   moan
loudest   when
passing   through
my throat?
An esophagus   where my
mother   tongue
was spoken   seldomly.
Let me try   to   breathe
in   and   out
before you   choke me
and fill these   lungs with
curses   and spells.
Inhabit   me,
fill me with   fear,
jealousy.   If there
can   only
be   one,
let it not be me.

Child

When fucking this thing I am—
rough bites and cuts
swelling with blood,
this body is unforgiving.
 Vindictive.
 Vicious.
 Vile.
—Unwilling to bear life.

Reckless

I've always been reckless

with the way I let men crash
into me
strangers tasting a chest
that I grew with care
sliding his
hands into my body

~~why are his nails so sharp?~~

I think I've been reckless

be gentle
I've told him
grab my hair, flip me over
they never listen
fuck me drunk, tear me open

~~I bled into my sheets that night~~

I know I've been reckless

this body I never asked for
touched

~~they never asked either~~

I've been reckless

because men

are reckless with me.

Under Uprooted Trees

There are days
where I don't
remember my name,
losing track of
who I am now
and what I was.

A husk of faux
masculinity,
toxicity,
this shell of
a man who
never existed.

Losing control
of names chosen
and names given,
losing track of
selves I killed,
buried under
uprooted trees.

VACANT

I am not in the world today.
I left this cage of a chest
open in winter
my body, still shining

        NO VACANCY
              above my abdomen.

They always told me this body is mine,
that autonomy is key

           breakdown, undone

I can destroy it freely
so, I will.

I will snap my limbs
suck the marrow from

                my hungry bones
          and fill those hollow spaces

                      with

you.

I will gut myself
      with hooks made of hands
            flood the
            floorboards with
              tears
           of fluoride and flora

build enamel

plant seeds

and hope that
something grows.

break my jaw

in emptiness

C(um) Etiquette

Some days I leave my window open.
Some days it's to   air out the smell of   you.
Some days it's to lure you in with the scent of me.
I don't know how to navigate this etiquette
of coming   and going,
the ways we invite strange bodies into our lives
expecting   something different
than this
godless fucking.
Some days I wish you would tear me apart.
Some days I want   to feel nothing
but you,   moving inside of me.
Some   days
I come/cum   and you go

—*don't come back.*

Cold

I promise
I am used to
the   cold.
It's in the wind
the   water
the way my love left me
in the place, she died alone.

It was in me
            through lust,
            loss.

Nights spent with men
                    frozen
my breath, heat on
necks, melting
into a puddle
in the middle of a bed
                    where I was alone.
It was in me
as I lay in an empty bank
            drunk
clinging to a man who
                    wasn't mine.
Betrayal couldn't thaw me
but it was warm,
                    for a moment.

The Girls

I can flirt ferociously with lust
spit fire of cautious songs
pulsing with hormones and rage
that I acquired over time
I am intimidating to you, of course
I should be, as I am visions of a woman
you are told not to have
/canthave/
I am the kind of girl you jerk off to
under the covers in your dorm room
while your cute cis white blonde skinny girlfriend is away
I am the kind of girl you match with on tinder
/againandagain/
left, left, right, left, right, repeat
swiping so you can ask these questions and validate
/dirtyfuckingdesiresdaddyhadtoo/
these girls you crave, pumping out cum
like lotion to moisturize the dryness of
a yearning pushed onto you
/soboringsobland/
I am the kind of girl you pick up in your car at three in the morning
looking for a quick fuck, a goddess without a name
/trannyslutsaresoeasyright?/
when in reality it's boys like you who make us hard
boys like you who make us feel unlovable, a biological mistake
a game, an experiment, an experience, alive, afraid
I am the kind of girl you take on dates in dark rooms

back of bars where only rats will see her beauty
and in these dark caves you are kind
/Imissthisboyinthedark/
here I learned darkness is safer than light
because light makes boys like you
/leavethegirlslikeme/
I am the kind of girl you found love with in those dark holes.
love that you abandoned for being too much
too trans? too brown? too fat? too femme? too tall?
I am the kind of girl who knows I am too much
the kind of girl you left so she can find you in someone else
someone who can handle the women oozing from this body you loved
/toomuch/
I am the kind of girl that you continue to fuck behind curtains
in a bed where you are gentle and caring
/whatareyouthinkingrightnow?/
because I can't stop thinking about when you left me
for strawberries and cream, even though caramel is sweeter
for that woman who's easier to control, easier to love
/butintheendyoufuckedusboththesame/
I am the kind of girl who learned my boundaries by dating you
because you crossed them and built them up like a wall
/funnyisntit?/
that your white bodies are so used to building and tearing down at will
funny that your sex feels like colonization in this body I called home
/andisthiswhattruelovefeelslike?/

because I became this girl who stopped showing up at three in the
    morning
The girl who knows I am not a secret
The girl who finds pleasure through open windows
The girl who is more desirable than fuckable
The girl you won't have
The girl you can't have
The girl who was intimidating
The girl in dark rooms
The girl with many names
The girl full of estrogen and rage
The girl who loved you even behind those curtains
And the girl who loved herself more than men
but that scares you
—*it should.*

In Dying I Become

Death is a ceremony
loss of a *son*
                    brother
mourning a body
never whole
never mine

give me
an offering of tobacco
burn these lungs
help me pass
push me forward

In dying I become

this ocean
mother ran to
the water
that birthed a
daughter

washed away
with waves of
forgiveness
to destroy all
evidence

In dying I become

eulogy of selves
gutted and rotten
boys lost in forests
those playgrounds
those seas
those places
never seen

words written
to welcome and dismiss
two selves
not whole, not mine
not quite yet

In dying I become, *reborn*.

Brother

Your wedding day was a hurricane; your bride in red was like a kiss on the dry prairie dirt. You actually never told me the story of how it went. The wedding, I mean. In fact, you never told me about how you chose a DJ, or if the flowers glistened in the sunlight. I don't think you've ever told me about the places you would love to see, either, or the way our dad smelled when you were seven. I never heard about the night you fell in love, or the days you fell in pain. I didn't hear from you the night your mother died, or when our dad left you too. I don't know where you grew up, or if you grew up next to me on that same dusty rez. I didn't hear the stories of your triumphs and failures, how you loved math as a kid and smoked too much weed in middle school; did you drop out or did you graduate top of your class? You never indulged in telling me stories the way brothers do. You didn't teach me how to shave, or how to talk to girls. In fact, I never learned how to talk to girls; even now, I can barely talk to myself. You never had the chance to keep me safe from rez dogs or take me home from that party where I got too high. But there are things I never told you, either. Like how I loved a boy, and I know, I know it's hard to hear that your brother was gay, but I fixed that too. You never actually had a brother, and your sister is straight, for the most part. I never got to tell you about the time when that boy broke my heart. I'll never tell you about how the ocean feels on my skin, or that I didn't know you existed until I was already across the country. I'll never give you the pieces to find me, or tell you that maybe I could be a poet, a sculptor of words. And I will never tell you that for me, your wedding day was a hurricane.

Berries

Do you remember the sweetness
of freshly picked berries
between the reservations, the cities,
open land, seemingly untouched by white hands?
I wish I could've seen the blood in the dirt,
the pink in our saliva, dripping on pale shirts.
I wish I could've seen the death in the grass,
the bones in our high cheeks, the mother in those seeds.

Residential

Resonance of a complex.
The complex being
this space.
Resonance,
this existence.

The traumas reverberate
vibrating on my rib cage
Punnichy bruised under my breasts.
This pain will echo through me
to my urban children
born by fire, fuelled with love.

I will sing them something beautiful
teach them how to speak

Nêhiyawêwin along Highway 15.
Gordon Indian Residential School
was only killed in '96
two years after my resurrection,
may they know the history
without the scars.
Ay-hay, Kokum
Ay-hay, Mother
for not letting the incendiary of womanhood
be extinguished by this body.

Chords

I live in a city
where you can hear
whales sing,
siren songs

reverberating
off lonely chords.
Songs I will sing back
in a harbour

familiar with the brown
of the wood
resembling the cracks of
my own skin.

I can read them like
the bottoms of my rough
Indian feet.

They say, take me home:
The prairies sing too.

Rain

I longed to see vast oceans
in blue eyes, frozen daggers
blinding as he entered me

open seas not ventured
beauty in an icy death

but I found the sun in yours.
Brown, looking into mine
as you drank my lips.

I wondered if our ancestors
would love us in this moment

if they could hear beating
from your chest, as I kissed it
how the rain and your body
sang for more.

I will hear that song
until we meet again.

Mother/Creator

Creator,

                  I want you to know that I'm trying

to cultivate

               to create

      to learn   but I forget how

to know I have not given up

           I will remember in prairies

what you left in my throat

                  I will sing with no voice

                           no language

                           no song

      can you hear it

Mother,

        I don't know if I can do this

       can I process

                    can I forget

          can I be whole

can I be holy

                   'cause I know

      I can't breathe

               with these broken ribs

Bear

There is so much
I don't know
about the potholes and prairies
inhabiting parts of my body,
this missing crevice of my groin
untouched by brown hands,
white men leaving bodies bruised.

There is so much I can't speak
with this tongue longing to see
if colonization tastes the same on you.
If I kiss the tears off your face
will I remember the salt in mine
and forgive them?

Will I remember another life?
Where I don't have to ask in English:

Could you feel this longing too?

Who Will Save You Now?

*"Your white cisgender boyfriend can't save you from the
end of the world."*
—Kai Cheng Thom

Who can save you now that the boy is
off loving someone less complicated?

A body not tarnished with
something extra
white skin like his parents
and their parents before them

ancestors who locked ours in buildings
we burned to the ground.

Who will save you now that your homelands
hate the holiest parts of you?

Queerness and indigeneity not intersecting quietly
white queers policing your existence
indigenous blood telling you that you're
a new generation problem.

Who will save you now that your sisters
live half a continent away?

While these men choke you
beat you in bathroom stalls
crush your ribs against brick walls
in queer bars, downtown home.

Who will save you now if you can't save yourself?

Is This My Home?

Is this my home?

Is it the fields of yellow where I was taught isolation and fear, where I imagined her dancing with coyotes, twisting and turning in the never-ending fields of flowers and grass? Is it those same wide-open spaces where my ancestors thrived in their magic only to have it ripped from their scalps? Is it the city where I spent my childhood realizing my brown skin was less than yours and hearing stories of how you cut her hair after she tried to run away from you? Is it the place where you spit on my bloodline in disgust because of what you made us out to be, and where my mother fled from with her children? Is it the land where I traded my fields of yellow for never-ending blue sky, where I taste the salt water on my lips like my kokums before me tasted their own blood? Is it the roads littered with potholes and gravel that got caught in my cut-up knees, burning and slicing as you called me a faggot? Is it the school where you filled me with sweet cum and sour words because I craved your approval and you craved my body? Is it the place where I met that boy and gave him my adolescence, or the brook where he ripped out my heart and I filled the space with burning alcohol and ashy cigarettes? Is it the bar where I spun in circles, dancing not with coyotes but with snakes and thieves that made me feel alive but stole my will to live? Is it the bathroom where you put your hands up my skirt as I pushed you away and you told me, *A girl like you shouldn't be saying no*? Is it the place where I couldn't get out of bed after you fucked me, because I knew you were just another white boy I thought could love me? Is it the place I ran away to with my indigenous sister I met in the system that failed us both? Is it the city where we roamed, running through fountains during storms when we had nowhere to be and no one to care? Is it the community I found, of black and brown femmes who make me feel safe and whole? Is it the family I stumbled upon in a drunken and violent rage to become something else, someone else? Where I reclaimed the femme magic of my kokums and where I too tasted my own blood? Is it the fields of yellow where I can't see her dancing anymore, those same wide spaces my people still die for, or that city I will never return to?

Is this my home?

Born in Mourning

I was born in the setting sun
prairie dusk, early mourning.
Named after the dead
Cree man killed in a bar
                        Saskatchewan.

I am the grief, the lost son
reborn, destined to die young.
My auntie told me,
I can see him in your eyes.
Fuck, I hope he's still there.

I was born in a rising moon,
grieving before I could walk.
I could only cry in Cree,
for the bodies like mine.

Why do I have a body like mine?
A body to be chewed through,
discarded into water.
Will I be reunited
in the tears of my creator,
see my mushum sob,
let him hold me like the day he died?
I was born in the setting sun,
alone with my mother, who whispered,
It's just you and me against the world

'cause she always knew the world
wanted me dead.

Newfoundland

I.
I often think
about baths
shared together
in distance
songs shared
guitar played
with fingers, you run
through my hair
lips dripping
intoxication
as you put your body
in mine
the first time.
Beer and cum
all I tasted
as you kissed me
goodbye
and I watched
you leave.

II.
gone
islands of
waves and rocks
consume space

     between us

communication
over screens
snapshots a life

     that's not us

this place you
call home
this girl you
call mine

     it's not me

I delete
the evidence
~~baths shared~~
~~guitar played~~
~~beer and cum~~

     gone

like the space
between *us*

III.
Can you grieve
men who are
still here
wanting to
fuck you
fill you
with their bodies
that you pretend
were lost
in an ocean
that kept you
apart?
Can you grieve
a ghost
you killed in
~~jealousy~~
let them
~~eat~~ you
~~taste~~ you
~~savour~~ you
in their mouth?
Are you allowed to grieve
for the girl
this man loves
the girl he sleeps
next to

instead of you
as he fucks you
in her bed?
Can you grieve
men who are
still here
fucking you?

Date #1

I gave you head after we finished our drinks

s a l i v a
o n
s a l t
o n
s k i n

I was eager to please a stranger in the dark
messy room, cramped couch.
You reached for the never-ending space
between my legs and I pulled away,

D o n ' t
D o
T h a t

I said, and you finished in my mouth.

I Am the Boundless Space between Oceans of Water and Wheat

I.
Kokum,
can I tell you
that this land feels like a dream?
Something   untouched
by my skin
though she birthed me
beneath her fields   flowers and grass.
These memories feel like they're pulled
from pasts I absorbed through my leaves
a sort of photograph derived through photosynthesis
where you are the sun
                    the water
                    the air.

Kokum,
can I say
I can't recognize her face?
But maybe my body can recall
how her curves rocked me
                              to sleep?

That I dreamt of
myself wearing a yellow gown
dancing through her canola?
That I can see her ghost in Gordons,

waving goodbye
the first time   the last time.

Kokum, did I ever tell you—
the two places I slept best
were next to you
and next to her?

II.

Nana,

Can I call you Migiju? Can I speak Mi'kmaq?
Because even with this twisted Cree tongue,
I sang a song when you passed.
I don't know the words,
but the beat is a memory
your son taught me
to sing.
So, I will sing.

I will sing to the   birch trees,
watch their skin   peel
in   January.
Feel my skin   sliding,
waiting   for   it
to   fall   off   too.

I will sing to the   brook,
vocalize stories   shared
of a childhood,   jumping
into her.   A childhood
wishing   I knew more.
Migiju, as I speak in Mi'kmaq
and cry in Cree—
can you forgive me?

While

It's been a while
since a calm rushed
against my palms.
The relaxation of reflection
unwinding of my mind
in sync with the movement of
fingers   that lay
next to your   fist.
Since such ease has graced these
salty,   swollen lips.
The way I gape my jaw
to let   you enter
throat becoming rusted,
losing   vocabulary,
and how I let a   man
into the revolving door
once   used as legs,
bucking along   keeping tempo.
Will you fuck me into
divinity   Daddy?
It's been a while.

MANIFEST

For Billy

I think I want us to be forever
'cause the cultivation   of this craft
has asked of us to bear children we did not want
to crack open our chests   for an audience
gazing into the veins of   each other's worlds
wondering how this   ecology survives.

I like to think it lives in swamps
the bogs I grew up on   the wetlands
that keep my lungs dripping in   melodrama
how sometimes, when I feel   emotions,
I can't tell if I am drowning or if I'm too full
of a divisive or maybe   indecisive
way of being.   That if this body
is up for grabs,   under scrutiny,
fill it with flowers,   gold and pearls
so, maybe for once, it will be seen as pretty.

And if we must survive,
which means we must write,

I'll weave you into a poem,
this art of quilting words.

I think that's the closest thing
I will ever feel to love.

Silent

Freedom is safety in its truest form, a luxury not ours.
I think I've found something
in the creases in your lips
the relaxation of your jaw.

Hold me, squeeze my chest
to yours and let
fear evaporate from my body.

Let me hear your breath
through every pore,
let me feel your heart pulse
through your neck
as I lie on your warm chest

finding safety in silence
safety in sleep.

Constellations

I haven't felt lovely
since I felt your lips
pressed against my body
unconquered territory
this thing called no man's land
lined with a galaxy of nerves
constellations discovered
traced with tongues
on the paper of my skin
sounds of sunbursts
mimicking moans of each other
your voice echoing through dimensions
oh, and did I mention
I loved you here
and I'll never forget
the way your orgasms
remind me of comets
shooting across the starry
skies of my chest
how you looked at me
while moons collided like our bodies
unruly, destructive
creating new worlds
in the fire of old ones

Fall/Spring

His kiss tasted like
dew on morning leaves.
I told him,

Spring feels like falling—like release
so let me go now before I break.

But he gave me kisses
as we fell into something
like love in spring.

Waves and Glass

For Benjamin

Your paintings fill the blank
white walls of my room in May.

They remind me of the chaos of movement.

Waves of shattered glass, ebbing above my bed,
are now inhabiting my dreams in the kindest ways.
They remind me to cover my sharpness in acrylic
paint, let pink settle in the bluest parts of my being
and try not to cut too deep, too fast.

Regain smoothness
from my jagged edges.
Rebuild pieces
of a stolen body.

Date #2

You told me you like to lose control.
So I handcuffed you
       laid you in my bed,
  as you thrusted into me
my throat was
       a rocking chair
       a wave
       a pendulum
       and you
the force
       always in control.

Claws

You told me that you
like my golden claws on your back.
Beauty is pain, I'm told,
so I melt and mould molten metallics
onto my nail bed—it burns at first
unbearable fires on my fingertips
are worth the way you look at me
with these extensions wrapped
around your body.

Your brown eyes meet mine as I kiss your groin
my blistered fingers don't feel pain.

Rework

I am reworking my reality.

  How does a tranny
co-exist
      with lust,
      being told of an
        "unattainable" touch
even with the saliva of a man
      dripping off my chest
      how he bites at
my soft parts
      and kisses me
      rigid?

I think this man
      could love me,
 fuck me
    outside of glory holes
     a bathroom stall
I think he could
 bring glory
      to all the empty holes
      in me
but still I'm stalling.
    Stutter.
      M a y b e
      I could love him too.

Maybe
     just,
        maybe

      my reality
is reworking me.

Iskwêw

For Nêhiyaw sisters

I buy my beadwork from
instagram, double-click
Nêhiyaw iskwêw
love the look of a
modern savage.

Kokum, be proud

because I have feathers longer
than my thick black hair
draping my chest now
and Cree is passing these red lips,
a violent shade, carnivorous.

Auntie, be proud

because I know there is learning to do
and I am patient, I promise
there is learning to do and I will try to unlearn
with you.

Mother, be proud

because I am the woman you raised through trial,
a difficult daughter born through sliced skin
held together, by that mattress on your
living room floor. The place I slept
when he left me, and I started to grieve this body.

Sister, be proud

because these children are pieces
of us, reflections of the people who died
they are beauty in rawness
cheekbones and lips
bright eyes, and rage.

Matriarch, be proud

I am sculpted for you.

OSCANA
For Kokum Shelly

One day, I'll return to the prairies
roam west to man-made reservoirs and
royal parks built on bones of bison
—Oscana Creek, Wascana Lake.

This city is a memorial and it will smell familiar
Big Gulps and cigarettes, the Queen City Ex
I will tell stories of how I got these scars
from slides, burns me and my sister still share.

I will come home, to kiss my kokums goodbye
and ask if they recognize this face
changed by estrogen and fear
tell them kîmiyosiw, the ocean and the transition.

I hope they think it was beautiful too.

Acknowledgments

PRISM international—"D/REAM ME" (Fall 2018)
This Magazine—"Rework" (Fall 2018)

Ay-hay, Mother and Father, for being able to learn and unlearn—your love is a gift I've taken for granted. I hope you're proud.

Ay-hay, Brian, Robert, Shirarose, Cynara, Oliver and the whole team at Arsenal Pulp Press for sending this book lovingly into the world.

Ay-hay, Billy, for agreeing to edit this collection—as you said in the mountains, *our friendship is old and ancient.*

Ay-hay, Saige, for sharing your incredible artwork, talent and friendship with me.

Ay-hay, Carmella and Alex, *the holy trinity.* We are incendiary.

Ay-hay, MH, FE, KT, HC, SP, CT, AS, RD, LD and LAP—these initials mean more to me than you know.

Ay-hay, Christine, for reading these poems again and again and again—you kept the fire burning.

Ay-hay, Catherine, Trish, Casey, Alicia, Joshua, Zoe, Emma, Erica, Lindsay, Dayna, Jeremy, Rebecca, Vivek, Alok, Jia qing, Jaye, Hannah, Alex, Rosanna, Kama, Lou, Brielle, Sarah, Stefanie, Keltie, Tara, Merray, Brandon, Cassie, Amber, Deirdre, Melody, Jessica, Tenille,

Delilah, Nikki, Daniel, Farzana, Emily, Rhiannon, Jade, Cory, Erin and everyone else who has shown me kindness, welcoming and warmth during this journey.

Ay-hay, my Indigiqueer and Two-Spirit kin, this is for us.

Photo: Laurence Philomene

ARIELLE TWIST is a writer and sex educator from George Gordon First Nation, Saskatchewan, based out of Halifax, Nova Scotia. She is a Nêhiyaw, Two-Spirit, trans femme supernova writing to reclaim and harness ancestral magic and memories. Within her short career pursuing writing she has attended a residency at Banff Centre for the Arts and Creativity and has work published with *Them*, *Canadian Art*, *The Fiddlehead* and *PRISM international*. *Disintegrate/Dissociate* is her first book. ***arielletwist.com***